Meet Me at the Hipster Apocalypse

Devin Sheehy

Porkopolis Productions

Cincinnati, Ohio

DEVIN SHEEHY

MEET ME AT THE HIPSTER APOCALYPSE

DEVIN SHEEHY

MEET ME AT THE HIPSTER APOCALYPSE

DEVIN SHEEHY

MEET ME AT THE HIPSTER APOCALYPSE

DEVIN SHEEHY

MEET ME AT THE HIPSTER APOCALYPSE

DEVIN SHEEHY

MEET ME AT THE HIPSTER APOCALYPSE

MEET ME AT THE HIPSTER APOCALYPSE

MEET ME AT THE HIPSTER APOCALYPSE

DEVIN SHEEHY

MEET ME AT THE HIPSTER APOCALYPSE

DEVIN SHEEHY

MEET ME AT THE HIPSTER APOCALYPSE

DEVIN SHEEHY

MEET ME AT THE HIPSTER APOCALYPSE